MW01061231

Leprechauns, castles, good luck, and laughter.
Lullabies, dreams, and love ever after.
Poems and songs with pipes and drums.
A thousand welcomes when anyone comes...
That's the Irish for you!
— Author unknown

IRISh
Inspirations

Stories and Wisdom That
Celebrate the Magic of
the Emerald Isle

Edited by Angela Joshi

Blue Mountain Press™
Boulder, Colorado

We wish to thank these authors for permission to reprint the following poems in this publication: Elizabeth Reynolds for "Love at First Sight." Copyright © 2010 by Elizabeth Reynolds. Pat Flanagan for "Irish Kindness and Hospitality." Copyright © 2010 by Pat Flanagan. Dana Pearson for "One More Day." Copyright © 2010 by Dana Pearson. Katherine Klein for "Patsy." Copyright © 2010 by Katherine Klein. Kate Murphy Oakley for "Moved by the Music." Copyright © 2010 by Kate Murphy Oakley. Peggy Sjöström for "Coincidence and Courage." Copyright © 2010 by Peggy Sjöström. Joe Pasternak for "True Love in Inis Mór." Copyright © 2010 by Joe Pasternak. Annmarie B. Tait for "Mom-Mom's Irish Soda Bread." Copyright © 2010 by Annmarie B. Tait. Sarah Tuttle for "Being Irish Is a Blessing." Copyright © 2010 by Sarah Tuttle. Denice Ryan Martin for "A Drop of Irish." Copyright © 2010 by Denice Ryan Martin. Brendan P. Myers for "There Are No Strangers." Copyright © 2010 by Brendan P. Myers. Rosemary Dolan Lesh for "Food, Music, and Friends from the Old Country." Copyright © 2010 by Rosemary Dolan Lesh. Herb Shallcross for "Some Things Never Change." Copyright © 2010 by Herb Shallcross. Gina Wynne for "Rush Hour." Copyright © 2010 by Gina Wynne. Beth Wallach for "In an Irish State of Mind." Copyright © 2010 by Beth Wallach. A. G. McEvoy for "Romancing a Stone." Copyright © 2010 by A. G. McEvoy. Sheelagh McKay for "Childhood Memories in White Park Bay." Copyright © 2010 by Sheelagh McKay. Donna Duly Volkenannt for "Coming Home." Copyright © 2010 by Donna Duly Volkenannt. Diane Loftus for "Inheriting Irish Values." Copyright © 2010 by Diane Loftus. All rights reserved.

Library of Congress Catalog Card Number: 2009031265
ISBN: 978-1-59842-463-8

Library of Congress Cataloging-in-Publication Data

p. cm.
ISBN 978-1-59842-463-8 (trade paper : alk. paper) 1. Ireland—Social life and customs—Anecdotes. 2. Ireland—Description and travel—Anecdotes. 3. National characteristics, Irish—Anecdotes. 4. Ireland—Miscellanea. I. Joshi, Angela, 1976-
 DA925.I7414 2010
 941.5—dc22

                                                                                2009031265

Blue Mountain Arts, Inc.
P.O. Box 4549, Boulder, Colorado 80306

Contents

Introduction

Ireland is known by many names: the Emerald Isle, Erin, Eire, the Land of a Thousand Welcomes, the Land of Saints and Scholars. But no matter what you may call it, one thing about Ireland always holds true: it is a place of beauty, magic, and rich cultural tradition that charms its inhabitants and visitors alike.

Irish Inspirations beautifully captures all the enchantment of Ireland with personal essays from locals, people of Irish descent, and tourists who've visited the land and fallen in love with it. Each essay celebrates various aspects of the country and culture—from the breathtaking forty-shades-of-green landscape to the unparalleled friendliness of its people; from the important values passed down from Irish ancestors to its traditions of music, food, dance, and literature. All have earned Ireland its many names and make it the special place that it is.

If these stories and essays share a common message, it is that Ireland leaves an indelible impression on the heart.

So whether you are Irish, love the Irish lifestyle, or are simply interested in learning more about the Emerald Isle, the stories and wisdom in this book will inspire you, put a smile on your face, and add a wee bit of Irish to your life. *Sláinte!*

Love at First Sight

by Elizabeth Reynolds

y first love was not a man, but a country. And she was an enigma, at that. When we initially met, she insisted upon being referred to by various names, including (but not limited to) Eire, Erin, and... perhaps you've heard of this one... Ireland. As far as first impressions go, I thought she was wild. Maybe she wasn't the kind of girl you'd want to bring home to your mother, but if you were like me, you'd do it anyway. You would put Erin first. You would choose her over anyone. That was the kind of power she had. She was charming and kind and beautiful enough to break a person's heart. Her land could seduce anyone, with raging waves crashing against tired coastlines and hills and valleys so deep and so blindingly green that you'd have to squint your eyes against the color.

Each city was unique, so different from the last, all of them brimming with energy and life and love. In Dublin's Temple Bar district, people danced in the streets. I think they would've moved to music even if there hadn't been any. They would've made their own. In Galway's Eyre Square, teenagers shared crisps and chips with each other and talked excitedly about their favorite bands or the latest ridiculous thing that their parents said. They were in love with each other, and they were in love with Erin, too. Everyone was.

I walked along her shores and sidewalks carrying an umbrella in my hand for three weeks, yet the rains never came. I awoke every day to a stream of sunlight pouring through the windows and a shock of blue sky. Birds sang for me in this country. The stars shone so brightly at night that it was like living in heaven. Rainbows lit up the sky above the Shannon River, and I instinctively knew that if there could ever be a pot of gold at the end of one of these things, it would have to be here. (It probably wouldn't have taken much to convince me of fairies or mermaids in this place either.) Erin was pure and utter magic.

Don't get me wrong; she's had her share of troubles. People have lost their lives fighting over her, and they've made sacrifices for her that will never be forgotten. Her soil has been stained by too many tears to count, and we must never forget her history. We must not use it as a divide either. Instead, we must learn from it. After all, Erin is nothing if not a good teacher.

I haven't been back to see Erin in a while. The years slip by so fast that they're almost impossible to catch, but I think about her all the time. So if any of you get to see her before me, please tell her that I haven't forgotten her. Tell her that my love for her is still unwavering. And tell her that I'll be coming home soon.

Anyone who has the pleasure of experiencing the magic and beauty of Ireland is truly a fortunate soul.

Irish Kindness and Hospitality

by Pat Flanagan

h, you'll love Ireland," our friends all said. "The Irish are so friendly." Nowhere was this truer for my husband and me than after touring Dysert O'Dea Castle one day just outside of Corofin. As we were leaving we noticed that we were out of gas. Heading back into the castle, we explained our problem to the woman at the ticket counter.

"Oh, you poor dears," she said. She paused for a second and then said, "My husband will help you. He's at home right now having his lunch, but he'll drive you to the nearest petrol station."

With that she gave us directions for how to walk to her home. "Just tell my husband that Mrs. Hanlon sent you. He'll see to your troubles." So off we went.

We approached the front door and paused. Here we were in a foreign country about to ask a perfect stranger to let us into his home and take time out of his day to drive us to the nearest petrol station and back to our car because his wife said he would. We knocked, and Mr. Hanlon opened the door. We explained our problem and his wife's offer to help. He never blinked an eye at the obligation that had been pressed upon him. "Aye, just wait 'til I've finished my tea and my newspaper, and I'll take you to Corofin."

Once Mr. Hanlon had finished his tea, he grabbed his newspaper and a plastic gas container. We drove to the petrol station and then back to the castle, thinking we'd soon be on our way. But there was one problem: no nozzle on the gas container and no way to get the gas into the tank without spilling most of it on the ground. Now what?

Well, it seems newspaper is a versatile material. Mr. H. took his paper, rolled it into a funnel, and in no time we had a full tank. With smiles of relief and handshakes all around we got ready to depart. We tried to give him a couple of pounds for his trouble, but he refused the money. We pressed. He refused again. It was only when we said, "Here, have a couple of pints on us," that he finally relented.

This experience reminded me of something a French traveler who toured all over Ireland in 1644 remarked in his journal: "The Irish are very fond of strangers." We'll drink to that!

The Irish: be they kings or poets or farmers,
they're a people of great worth.
They keep company with angels
and bring a bit of heaven here to earth.
— Irish saying

One More Day

by Dana Pearson

 was in Ireland for a week with my best friend, Bob. Rather than spend our time on a bus surrounded by tourists, we decided to rent a car and set out on our own, which turned out to be a smart decision.

Along the way we stumbled upon crumbling castles and one-room museums that were not listed in our guidebooks. We drank pints with the locals in tiny, out-of-the-way pubs, and we were even invited into a stranger's home for a traditional Irish breakfast. We got lost. We were rained upon. We made friends. For a week we simply wandered. In that time we hit all the major destinations, from the Cliffs of Moher to the Ring of Kerry, but we moved at our own pace and enjoyed the small treasures just as much as the large ones.

Our return flight was scheduled to depart at 4:45 p.m., and we milked our final day for all it was worth. After stopping for every excuse we could think of, we reluctantly returned the rental car and boarded the shuttle bus to the airport. We arrived an hour before our departure time and went immediately to the check-in counter.

"I am so sorry, gentlemen," said the clerk upon checking our reservations, "but that flight has been overbooked and, unfortunately, all the seats have been taken."

"I guess we'll just take the next flight then," I replied as I looked to my friend, who nodded in agreement.

"Well," answered the clerk, a look of dread crossing his face, "the thing is, you see, that was the last flight of the day to your destination. I am so sorry."

"Are you trying to tell us," asked Bob as he stepped forward, "that we will be spending one more night in Dublin?"

"Having one more Irish breakfast?" I added.

"Drinking one more Guinness?" continued Bob.

"Uh... just *one* more Guinness?" I asked, looking sideways at my friend.

We both laughed. We had one more day. The clerk looked relieved. Oh, the luck of the Irish.

The man who has luck in the morning
has luck in the afternoon.

— Irish saying

Traditional Irish Toasts

May green be the grass you walk on,
may blue be the skies above you,
may pure be the joys that surround you,
may true be the hearts that love you.

May you always have walls for the winds,
a roof for the rain, tea beside the fire,
laughter to cheer you, those you love near you,
and all your heart might desire.

May the lilt of Irish laughter
lighten every load.
May the mist of Irish magic
shorten every road...
And may all your friends remember
all the favors you are owed!

May you get all your wishes but one,
so that you will always
have something to strive for!

Hooked on a Single Place

by *Christine S. Cozzens*

 friend who has been traveling to China since the '70s stood with me on a terrace overlooking the yellow-tiled roofs of Beijing's Forbidden City, a vast maze of buildings and courtyards organized to follow the points of the compass and the contours of the land.

"Every time I come to Beijing, I come here first," she explained, then paused, searching for words. "And my mind just... goes."...

I was lucky to have her as a guide on my first trip, China-addict that she was. Though not of Chinese ancestry, from her studies and her many trips, she had come to live and breathe the country and is happiest, she tells me, when she has her feet on its soil.

Another friend flies off to Mexico constantly, even for a long weekend, on the flimsiest of excuses. She goes often enough to have a complete second life—perhaps a second self—at her hillside cottage in Oaxaca.

Still another worked several summers in Lugano, Switzerland, and kept going back even after the job ended. Every summer when her stay is over, the proprietors of her favorite restaurant give her a going-away party with the dishes and wines she prefers.

These women are not dispossessed natives or roots-seekers; none has ethnic ties to the country of her obsession, though such connections drive many travelers. They all seem to have caught their passion by intellectual accident: a book, a course, a trip taken at a moment of vulnerability or openness.

I know the feeling. I spent a bone-chilling March week hitchhiking around Ireland in 1971, and somewhere between negotiating the dark confusion of pre-Celtic Tiger Dublin and biking along the serene lakes of Killarney, I got hooked. Though I love many places and make it a point to travel to new ones, I live and breathe Ireland and mark my life by which trip I'm planning or remembering.

Familiarity amid strangeness casts an addicting spell. It feels good to be known and to know your way around, especially in a place where you are a guest and can savor the sweet ordinariness of daily life in a way that is simply not possible at home. To sit on the same old bench on St. Stephen's Green in Dublin (we call it Stephen's Green over there), sipping a Bewley's coffee and watching toddlers throw bread to the ducks—this is happiness. From endless walking at all hours of the day, I know the streets of Dublin and Belfast better than I do those of Atlanta, where I live but am always driving somewhere in a rush.

When I'm traveling in Ireland, I have the leisure and the mental tenacity to explore: back alleys, grocery stores, doorways, and neglected buildings are somehow more interesting than the ones I see every day at home. In Dublin, I even have a favorite pub, the Old Stand, where I'm a "regular," though I only drop in once or twice a year.

This rush of familiarity grips me in haunts all over the country. From Sligo to Schull, Galway to Avoca, routine walks take me to beloved views, past favorite shops and restaurants, and over ground that recalls other trips, other years: the hotel restaurant in Gort where my kids ate two huge dishes of apple crumble each and my nine-year-old daughter, Emma, told the waitress, "Send my compliments to the chef"; the shop on Achill Island where I bought yarn for my first Aran sweater and learned how to do a cable stitch; the view from a beach on the Dingle Peninsula of Great Blasket Island. Each new trip adds a layer to these memories and a little more knowledge to my lifelong project of understanding Ireland...

But the yearning for familiarity and for the easeful retracing of steps can't fully explain my desire to return again and again to the same country, the same routes and haunts. Like choosing a major in college or reading all the novels by a favorite author, my need to go back to Ireland has something to do with wanting to know a lot about one thing. It's important that the one thing be outside myself, beyond my daily experience, something I can see from afar.

To slake this thirst, I read every book or article about Ireland, past and present, that I can get my hands on; when I'm there, I listen to radio announcers, taxi drivers, and shop clerks and eavesdrop on bus or cafe conversations to fill in the rest. I am as interested in the varieties of Irish cheese, the latest government scandal, or which movie stars were spotted at the Leopardstown horse races as I am in the formal drama of Ireland's history and culture.

To try to know China or Oaxaca, Lugano or Ireland is at least an effort to gather the experiences and memories of a lifetime in one place. My fellow obsessives share my penchant for soaking up all kinds of knowledge about their chosen places, collecting books, newspapers, and other publications; they haunt online sites and discussion forums.

Each morning when I'm not in Ireland, I visit The Irish Times's Web site... for its Weather Cam to see what the weather and traffic look like at the O'Connell Bridge, an intersection I've crossed hundreds of times on foot. This voyeuristic moment gives me a taste of being there, a brief escape from the day that lies ahead.

Though each of us is in her own way an expert, for our pains we are subject to the friendly ridicule of friends, who laugh at our mastery of Chinese or Irish trivia yet want us to help them plan their trips. We forgive them readily, hoping that they, too, will one day be captured by a lurking passion for some piece of the planet.

We can never truly know these places we obsess about. But looking in from the outside helps us look back at ourselves—one way of finding our place in the world.

Patsy

by Katherine Klein

A map told me how to reach County Clare, Ireland, but a dog named Patsy made me welcome.

A few years ago, a friend and I borrowed a cottage in Moveen, a farming village near the craggy western coast. The cottage was comfortable and fixed up with modern conveniences—hot water, a kitchen, a stone floor, chests of sweaters. We didn't need the peat-burning fireplace to keep us warm or to make our tea and oatmeal that first morning, but the raindrops on the window reminded me that once this home had an earthen floor and the occupants had endured the long, northern winter nights with only small flames to keep them warm and give them light.

We walked to the sea after breakfast. The farmland looked unchanged for the past hundred years. We passed abandoned buildings; one barn was a heap of stones next to the foundation of a house whose occupants had moved on long ago.

We reached the sea and looked down the jagged shore to the rough, cold sea below. The night's rain had cleared, but low clouds raced across a bright sky. There was Bishop's Island, where monks once lived in solitary devotion. We could see the ruins of their hut. And there in the far distance was the western horizon and beyond it, America. This was the direction many residents of County Clare had taken years back, away from this place.

As we walked back to the cottage the clouds continued to blot the sky, mottling the land in sun and shade. We hadn't seen a soul. I started to think this place by the sea was a lonely place—lovely, but lonely.

Then we met Patsy. He raced out to meet us on our second walk—tongue lolling, black-and-white tail waving. Patsy, our neighbor's border collie, appointed himself our guide and guardian, and he changed my view of Moveen.

He didn't jump or bark, but greeted us politely. As we continued on our walk, he trotted alongside us for a bit. After making sure we were comfortable, he raced off on other business: There were horses in the pasture to the left; Patsy made sure they took a few brisk laps around. There were cows in the field to the right; Patsy corralled them in a tight circle and then trotted back to us, pleased with his work. Just then, a truck approached on the narrow road. We had to climb out of the road, but he raced to catch it. With so much to look after between his house and the sea, the dog didn't walk in a straight line for long.

We walked to the sea every day. Each time, Patsy met us on the road and continued with us to the shore, saying farewell only when we'd arrived back at his gate. His loyalty led to tea and friendship with his owner, a woman who had lived in the area all her life.

A dog named Patsy showed me the way to the sea and the way to see County Clare as it truly is—a vibrant corner of Ireland.

The best guide to a new place
may not have to say a word.

Moved by the Music

by Kate Murphy Oakley

In the 1980s, my brother, cousins, and I were school kids living the American Dream. The Top 40 was our soundtrack, and Irish music, our ancestors' music, existed on frequencies we had yet to hear. Then one summer, Grandpa Murph played an Irish Rovers record for us. We had never heard anything like these lively, interesting stories set to music. The songs begged us to dance round the living room, porch, kitchen, and back again. So we did, even after our cheeks turned ruddy and our legs floated from exhaustion. The heartfelt emotions and everyday details in those songs funneled a foreign culture straight to our house in Michigan.

Years later, I visited Ireland and got to hear Irish musicians sing more stories in pubs and on the radio. As they channeled their gift of gab into songs, I realized the Irish have another, less noted gift—that of listening. They write and sing about things people easily connect to because they first connect to people.

I began really listening to these new songs and stories. Sometimes they reminded me of my family and drew me into the past. Sometimes they surprised me with lyrics that revealed more about what it means to be Irish. In many ways, I felt like I was dancing once more around my grandparents' living room, happily following unfamiliar songs.

Nothing makes you want to dance more
than an Irish song sung from the heart.

A Round of Songs
at a Pub in Rosscarbery

by Tom Coyne

round the table the songs went—a more melodious "Fields of Athenry," and a second rendition of "Forty Shades of Green"—before an old man in a Hawaiian shirt interrupted a cup of tea to give us his best "Spancil Hill." The bartender's mother arrived, short black hair and a decade younger than her husband sitting next to me. She kissed his cheek and looked over to the singers, rolling her eyes. Their son was with her, a twelve-year-old who ran for a tube of Pringles from behind the bar and showed up his sister by pouring his dad a near-perfect pint of Guinness, all while one singer handed off to the next, like a slow fuse sizzling its way down the bar toward me.

I didn't sing. But a tattooed forearm came over the shoulder of the mom now sitting next to me. "Come on, Mary, give us a song now."

She turned her face away from his breath and smiled at her husband. "Go on," he told her. And she started in with "My Old Man," as sentimental a song as I had ever heard. The room went quiet as she stared into a spot on the bar mat in front of her, and in a smooth falsetto made me wonder if it was okay for an American to cry at four o'clock in a pub in Rosscarbery. I used to think sappy folks who got emotional over sunsets and paperbacks and Daniel O'Donnell ditties were suckers; I was from a jaded country of the relentlessly sarcastic, a place where legends were for debunking, romance for exposing, the sentimental to be proven silly.

But as I watched the mother sing, and then her daughter taking her turn, reluctantly giving the room a song about lost love for a young Teddy O'Neill, eyes cast downward as she leaned against a row of bottles and sang, "*I see the old cabin beyond the wee boreen, I see the old crossroads where we used to dance. I ramble the lane where he called me his stoirin, and my girlish heart was so full of romance...,*" and I understood what I really loved about this country. The place had imagination, unchecked. It was sentimental and a sucker in the best sort of way. It was a place you could sing sappy songs in the afternoon, and rather than have to elbow your buddy and make a joke about the singer, you could just listen and let the hairs on your neck tingle, and then applaud.

There are two sides to every story
and twelve versions of a song.
— Irish proverb

Paying Tribute to Irish Ancestors

by Bruce Northam

n 1922, my grandfather, James O'Sullivan, a captain in the fight for Ireland's independence, emigrated from Ireland to the United States via Canada—one year after the partition of Ireland... He traveled west, laying Canadian rails, cowboy ranched in Montana, then hitchhiked to Manhattan's Upper West Side, where he opened and ran the popular O'Sullivan's Chophouse—in a neighborhood of Irish bars—for thirty-five years. Shortly after establishing himself in New York, his wife-to-be also emigrated from Ireland.

With that in mind, Mom and I visited Eire in tribute to her parents—and to see if the Irish would reciprocate the hitchhiking hospitality James O'Sullivan enjoyed in 1925 America.

In this land of fiercely independent people who value their poets as highly as their warriors, our strategy was to be road-warrior day-trippers and elegant country inn evening guests—upscale vagabonds. At first, she waved at cars to request rides, but the drivers only waved back. We needed a hitching sign, so I crafted four cardboard appeals: Mom, Angel, Innocent, and Pub, which worked best at small town intersections.

"So Mom, where should we venture today?"

"Never ruin a hike with a reason," she winked.

At that moment a car—piloted by an eighty-five-year-old woman—pulled over. We rode on narrow, stone-walled roads past thatched cottages, castles, fortresses, churches, and other noble dwellings. A prime-time radio talk show host mused about gardens and the comings and goings of birds in the yard... Then a "lost pet alert" was followed by a stolen bicycle appeal... The rain comes again. Our driver acknowledges, "The rain is fond of Ireland."

The landscape changed to sheer cliffs, wet meadows, rocky moonscapes, and roofless abbeys. We pass a damp, lush, lime-colored farm teeming with cattle... This enchanted Atlantic island foray reminded me of my mother's many traits—unconditional love, kindness, safety...

We were in for a shock—we are dropped off at a pub, even though we were picked up using the "Angel" sign. We ease into the social glue of pub life with a Guinness. Mom sits closer to the band playing music by the fireplace. Foot tapping gives way to knee slapping; soon she is dancing.

Then it dawned on me—the sign I forgot to make for her, representing what my mom stands for: Love.

"Wherever they may in the distance roam,
this country is never forgotten by its born."
— Barman looking over at my mother
doing the Irish jig to live pub music

Coincidence and Courage

by Peggy Sjöström

hen my husband and I visited Ireland, I had one of those "you've got to be kidding" experiences. You see, I've played folk music all my life—American old-time mountain music, bluegrass, coffeehouse folk, and even traditional Celtic music. A few years before going to Ireland, during our annual trip to Michigan to visit family and friends, we went to Lansing to do a bit of shopping at the mecca of acoustic instruments: Elderly Instruments. I bought an Irish drum, called a *bodhrán* (pronounced bo-rahn), that I wanted to learn to play for the occasional Irish tune we played in my folk-music band back in Sweden. When we got back home, I taught myself to play my new bodhrán the best I could, and for the most part it sounded pretty good.

So, after we had booked our flight to Dublin, I was surfing the Internet for special things to do while in Dublin. I happened to run across a music store called Waltons World of Music that offered private bodhrán workshops. I was thrilled with the idea of being able to take a lesson from a real Irish bodhrán player, so I booked a time for myself. I took my bodhrán with me, thinking that it might be smart to learn some advanced techniques using my own drum and "tipper" (drumstick).

Upon arriving for my lesson, I explained to my instructor that I had bought my bodhrán in Lansing, so he asked to look at it. He wanted to teach me the "anatomy" of the instrument and what to look for in a quality bodhrán. But as soon as he began to inspect the inside rim of it, his eyes widened and his jaw dropped. Why? Because the "label of authenticity" that was glued to the inside rim on my bodhrán has the words "Guaranteed Irish, by Waltons." He explained with an amazed look on his face that my bodhrán had been built in the basement of the very building we were in! I still get goosebumps to think that my bodhrán had "come home" in such an unbelievable journey—Dublin... Lansing... Sweden... and finally back to Dublin!

My lesson went very well, and my instructor encouraged me to find a real session (a music jam) somewhere in Dublin to join. I really don't know how I found the courage, but I did find and join a good session, which isn't as simple as just jumping in and starting to play. Oh, no... there's a whole set of unspoken rules and etiquette that must be followed. You have to sit "outside the circle" and listen to and observe the group for a while to first determine what style of music is being "accepted" by the group, the level of talent among the musicians, and who seems to be the leader. Musicians playing Irish music (whether they're Irish or American) can be pretty snobbish, so it's no easy task for a stranger who hasn't "earned his wings" to be welcomed into a session.

After following the rules of etiquette, I timidly took up my bodhrán from its case and very quietly started to play along.

I played for about an hour or so while my husband and I enjoyed a couple of beers. I actually got some attention from other listeners in the pub, and most "non-musicians" seemed to be interested in my playing. There were even some tourists who took my picture, probably because my bodhrán has a colorful Celtic pattern on it. (I discovered later that real bodhrán players would be ashamed to have any colorful design on their bodhráns!)

The musicians in the session completely and totally ignored me, which I figured was both good and bad. Bad, because it was probably obvious to the session musicians that I was an amateur and they didn't want to waste their time acknowledging my presence. Good, because I assume that I wasn't bad enough for them to throw me out of the session. Either way, I'm glad that I worked up the courage to sit in on a real Irish session in Dublin. It was a thrill I'll never forget!

May the sound of happy music
and the lilt of Irish laughter
fill your heart with gladness
that stays forever after.
— Irish blessing

The Best Outlook on Life

by Tom Coyne

I told my mother I wanted to retire to Ireland, because it seemed that white-haired people here didn't just curl up and expire. They danced. They laughed at bad jokes. They smiled, no matter that their smiles looked like they had divvied up a single set of teeth. Old men flirted with young women, old ladies sipped whiskey and giggled over the day's gossip. Farmers who looked like skeletons in their boots, people we'd put in a home, or maybe a box, spent their days working cattle. I walked the roads with them as they slowly made their way from field to field, herding dogs at their heels.

Their secret? Fresh air and fewer worries were my guess—maybe not fewer worries, necessarily, but the Irish didn't seem to possess the same sense of entitlement I was used to back home, the one that gave us the right to sit around all day and fret about our plight. Where I was from, the line between life and death seemed a negotiable one, so many of us spending most of our living hours trying to put off our dying ones. The Irish, they just got on with it, too busy to try to reorder the inevitable. You lived, worked, died, and laughed as much as possible along the way....

Dance as if no one's watching, sing as if no one's listening, and live every day as if it were your last.

— Irish proverb

A Bit of Irish Wisdom

A handful of skill is better than
a bagful of gold.

Don't be breaking your shin
on a stool that's not in your way.

You'll never plough a field by
turning it over in your mind.

Three best to have in plenty—
sunshine,
wisdom,
and generosity.

Patience is poultice for all wounds.

The future is not set; there is no fate
but what we make for ourselves.

God is good, but never dance
in a small boat.

A friend's eye is a good mirror.

Always remember to forget
the troubles that passed away,
but never forget to remember
the blessings that come each day.

Ireland's Literary Heritage

by Megan O'Reilly

In my native Chicago, where being Irish is akin to being a Cubs fan, I grew up going to St. Patrick's Day parades and eating corned beef and cabbage suppers. But later in life, reading is what opened my eyes to the real magic that is Ireland, a small island home to a disproportionate number of the world's most celebrated writers: James Joyce, William Butler Yeats, George Bernard Shaw, Samuel Beckett... and the list goes on.

Ireland is rich in tradition. Stretching back to medieval times, it is a country that has been beset by famine and political and religious strife. It is also a place of great beauty where coastal mountains surround central plains and a wet climate makes everything green and lush... and gray and chilly. These things combine to make Ireland a land of inspiration that breeds storytellers as plentiful in number as the sheep roaming its emerald hillsides.

There is Joyce, who wrote in *Ulysses*: "A man of genius makes no mistakes. His errors are volitional and are the portals of discovery." Yeats opined: "Education is not filling a bucket, but lighting a fire." Shaw said: "You see things; and you say 'Why?' But I dream things that never were; and I say 'Why not?'"

Like Ireland itself, so do these words inspire.

Just as geography can define its people, so can people define a place.

In Yeats' Footsteps

by Thomas Lynch

t was a poet who told me to go to Ireland. And poems that first made me want to go... The book I took with me was *The Collected Poems of W. B. Yeats*. It was a hardbound blue book with the author's monogram embossed in gold on the front cover. I had a few of the poems or portions of them off by heart.

> *When you are old and gray and full of sleep*
> *And nodding by the fire, take down this book*

Of course, I made the requisite Yeatsian pilgrimage, hitching to Kilrush and Ennis, thence north to Gort, then on to Coole Park to see the swans and the tree with the great man's initials in it and on to Ballylee where the ancient tower stands, albeit not in the ruins he predicted, with it's bridge and river, the broad green pasture, the hum of the motorway out of earshot, jackdaws diving from tree to tree. And carved on a stone there by his instructions, the inventory of "old mill boards and sea green slates/and smithy work from the Gort Forge," with which he had "restored this tower for my wife George"—the briefer line, the solid rhymes, the declarative confidence, like the music country people danced to. Lucky enough, I thought, to marry a woman named George—if only to rhyme her eventually with "Gort Forge."

I slept in Galway that night. Then on to Sligo, where, following the poet's instructions, under bare Ben Bulben's head, I found Drumcliff churchyard and the grave upon which I cast as cold an eye as I could muster, said my thanks, and went away. I walked around the Lake Isle of Innisfree, located the waterfall at Glencar and the rock at Dooney where the fiddler played.

I was young. Poets were my heroes. Where they'd been is where I wanted most to be.

So I wandered around Ireland as long as I could, night-portering in Killarney, learning to milk cows and manage dung in Moveen, reading Yeats and dreaming of the future, wondering what my true love's name would turn out to rhyme with.

Your feet will bring you
to where your heart is.
— Irish proverb

Crue Love in Inis Mór

by Joe Pasternak

oanne and I had just stepped down from the cart that was being pulled by a horse. It was a windy and slightly rainy day—typical Irish weather—as we began our trek from the cart up to the pathway in front of us. It was a path filled with jagged rocks and stretches of grass as far as the eye could see.

Even though she had never been up to Dún Aonghasa, Joanne had been to one of the other Aran Islands. She told me this one, Inis Mór, was the biggest of the three. We decided that we would visit the other two islands together in the future.

About halfway up the path, I turned around to take some pictures of the scenery. It was absolutely gorgeous. There was nothing like this back home in America that I could recall. The fact that there was so much history in Ireland drew me to it immediately. It made me smile to know that I was sharing this moment with someone I was extremely fond of.

"What are you smiling about, Joey?" she asked.

"Oh, just the view," I said. "This place is so serene. I love it."

"I'm glad you feel that way, *mo anam cara,*" she replied as she gave me a kiss and continued up the path.

Joanne was born and raised in Ireland on the east coast near Dublin. She was the epitome of the Irish culture. She had blonde hair, blue eyes, light freckles, and an accent to die for. Every time she would speak Irish to me I couldn't help but smile out of pure admiration.

We made it to the top of the path and passed through the stone formation of Dún Aonghasa. It has existed for over two thousand years, and it gave me a feeling of awe to be walking on the grounds of something that old. It was part of Ireland's identity and its rich history. I turned around and noticed the square patches of grass tightly hugging the stones from this height. I looked above me and saw the clouds moving around with the wind as it began to let up. The rain had ceased, and it looked like the sun was getting ready to shine.

I walked back to Joanne who was staring out toward the ocean. She pointed out to the left toward the Cliffs of Moher. The drop from the cliffs was a steep one, but the view of them was spectacular. When I saw that view, it made me realize how small and insignificant you can feel when you're standing beside a massive ocean. All the worries of the world seem to escape you and all you're left with is your thoughts.

Ireland had that impression on me. It might not be the sunniest and most temperate place in the world, but it does offer that escape to peace for me.

I took Joanne in my arms and held her tight as the sun poked through the clouds and shined down on us. I gave my Irish lass a kiss and smiled.

"Táim i ngrá leat," I said to her.

"I love you, too," she replied with a smile. *"Níl aon tinteán mar do thinteán féin,"* she added and gave me a tight embrace. She was exactly right: there really is no place like home.

It is in the shelter of each other that people live.

— Irish proverb

Mom-Mom's Irish Soda Bread

by Annmarie B. Tait

esterday I baked Irish soda bread. Over the years I imagine I've baked a hundred or more loaves of it. In fact, I believe I could close my eyes and make it without even thinking, but I never do. When the mood strikes me, the first thing I do is search out the tattered piece of paper on which my grandmother scratched down the recipe.

As I read it over yesterday and gathered the ingredients together, my mind drifted back to the stories I know by heart of how she and Pop-Pop met on the boat to America from County Cork, Ireland. I pictured her chestnut brown hair and blue eyes, the same hair and eyes I see when I look in the mirror.

I'm sure Mom-Mom didn't need a recipe to bake it. She learned how to make soda bread from her mother, as I learned how to make it from mine. Most likely she jotted down the recipe on a piece of paper so that some little bit of herself would be left behind in this world, to pass from one generation to the next. And so it went on to my mother, and it is now among my treasures where it will stay until it's my turn to pass it on. It may be a long wait. As of right now, I can't imagine parting with it.

Yesterday I gingerly unfolded the recipe and set it on the counter. After all these years, it is now yellowed with age and generously perfumed with the scent of caraway. The telltale sprinkling of smudges from spices and the like that have accidentally fallen onto the page over time only add to its character. Like a well-worn flag, this ragged slip of paper bears proudly the scars of its long and happy life.

The ritual continued as I gathered the ingredients and began to mix the dough. Over the years I've adapted the recipe to suit a modern-day kitchen, but the spirit with which I bake is centuries old. The essence of our Irish soda bread is the lilt in my grandmother's voice and the light in my own mother's eyes. This little scrap of paper I hold so dear awakened memories in me that can never be erased. What could warm a grandmother's heart more than that? Perhaps this was her intention all along.

As the bread baked, the aroma filled our house and I was transported back in time. I breathed in deeply and imagined myself as a schoolgirl once again, standing at my mother's side, learning the process of mixing the dough. Mom had a way of turning kitchen chores into a special kind of fun.

The minor adjustments I've made to the recipe have no great effect on the outcome. The finished product is delicious every time and to my way of thinking always tastes better to the keeper of the recipe than it does to anyone else.

The secret to enjoying the bread is knowing that you have the knack to make it come out just right. It's not because the recipe is perfect; it's not. But the spirit in the baking is. It's hard to spoil the taste of childhood memories. The love of my mother and grandmother saw to their sweet preservation.

A tradition passed down is an invisible thread that connects generations.

Irish Soda Bread Recipe

    4 cups all-purpose flour
    2 teaspoons salt
    2 teaspoons sugar
    2 teaspoons baking soda
    1 cup buttermilk

Preheat oven to 375°F. Lightly butter and flour a baking sheet and set aside.

In a large bowl, whisk together flour, salt, sugar, and baking soda. Form a well in the center and pour in buttermilk. With your hands (or a wooden spoon if you don't want to get too messy), mix just until you have a light dough.

Turn dough onto a lightly floured surface and form into a disc that is about 1 inch thick. Place the round onto the prepared baking sheet. With a sharp knife, cut a large X across the center of the dough and place in oven.

Bake for 45-50 minutes or until lightly browned and bread makes a hollow sound when gently tapped. Carefully remove bread from pan and place on wire rack. Serve warm with lots of butter!

rish soda bread became a staple of the Irish diet in the early to mid-1800s when sodium bicarbonate was first introduced to Ireland. It quickly became a bread that nearly every household regularly baked—traditionally in a black iron pot over an open peat fire. It is still a popular bread today, served at home and in pubs and enjoyed by tourists and locals alike.

Irish soda bread is traditionally made with just four ingredients: flour, baking soda, salt, and buttermilk. But there are many variations to the classic recipe. For a little more flavor, you can try adding caraway seeds, raisins, currants, orange zest, or herbs. (If you add raisins or currants, you'll have what's often referred to as a "spotted dog.") You can also use a combination of all-purpose flour and whole wheat flour to create a brown bread, which is also traditional in Ireland.

Why cut a cross or an X into the dough before baking? There are many theories as to how this tradition started. Some say it was to ward off evil, others that it was to "let the fairies out" while the bread was baking. Most likely, though, it simply helps the bread to bake more evenly. Plus, the cross acts as a good guide when you're ready to cut or break the bread before serving.

Bread tastes best when it's warm from the oven and shared among family and friends.

Irish Terms and Expressions

Sláinte (pronounced slawn-cha): Gaelic for "To your health" or "Cheers!"

Craic (pronounced crack): A Gaelic word that loosely translates to fun or enjoyment in the company of others. In Ireland you'll often hear expressions like "Let's go find the *craic*," "How's the *craic*?" or "The *craic* was mighty."

Blarney: Often referred to as the "gift of gab," blarney is more accurately defined as eloquence or skillful flattery. It is believed that if you kiss the blarney stone at the Blarney Castle near Cork, Ireland, you'll be endowed with this gift of eloquence.

The Full Irish: A traditional and very hearty Irish breakfast. Sometimes also referred to as a "fry-up," the Full Irish usually includes eggs, sausage, bacon rashers, potatoes, black pudding, white pudding, tomatoes, Irish baked beans, mushrooms, bread, and tea.

Blow-in: An Irish term for "someone who's not from around here." This term applies to foreigners who've settled in Ireland, as well as Irish people living in a different part of the country than where they were born. And once you're a blow-in, you're always a blow-in, no matter how long ago you "blew in."

The weather's gone soft: A phrase commonly used when it's about to rain or is raining lightly.

If you can see the hills, it's going to rain. If you can't see the hills, it's already raining: A comment on the frequency of rain.

Top o' the mornin' to you: Something they don't actually say in Ireland.

Being Irish Is a Blessing

by Sarah Tuttle

Walking into my great-grandmother's house, I was bombarded with Irish Catholic pride. John F. Kennedy and shamrocks adorned almost every wall.

I didn't always understand what was so great about being of Irish descent. To me, Ireland was a land of potatoes and leprechauns—both are well enough, but neither were cause for Saint Patrick's Day to be a national holiday.

One day, Great Grammy called me into her room. She patted the bed next to her and said, "It's like this, Sarah. Being Irish means we can face anything and believe that there's hope."

Now, years later, I stand by Great Grammy's gravesite. I sing softly along with my memory of her low, calming voice this Irish blessing for an Irish woman, from an Irish great-granddaughter...

May the road rise to meet you.
May the wind be always at your back.
May the sun shine warm upon your face and the rains fall soft upon your fields.
And until we meet again,
may God hold you in the palm of his hand.

A Drop of Irish

by Denice Ryan Martin

s a child, I frequently bemoaned my first name: Denice. It was a fussy French name that newly-arrived nuns or substitute teachers regularly mangled during attendance at Santa Maria del Popolo grade school.

"Dennis Ryan," they'd call from the lectern. No reply. "Dennis Ryan?"

"It's Denice." My meek response typically set off snickers up and down the classroom aisles.

Complaining to my mother about my first name was useless. She didn't apologize for the naming blunder. Instead she happily shared that she had the name Mary Lou picked out but changed her mind at the very last minute.

"I really don't remember why," she said. "If you don't like it, you can always take your middle name, Michelle. We can call you 'Mimi.'"

Oh, how I wished that Mary Lou had won out! As names go, it was not as pretty as Kathleen or Maureen, but it was surely one notch better than Denice (or De-nephew as kids liked to tease).

Thankfully, I was more than satisfied with my Irish last name: Ryan. It was short, easy to spell, and fairly common in our north Chicago suburb. Plus, I could legitimately wear a shamrock pin on St. Patrick's Day, unlike my Polish and German friends.

Or so I thought... until a homework assignment about my family tree shattered my cozy Irish-American picture.

"I'm 100 percent Irish, right?" I asked my Dad one evening at the kitchen table.

"No. You're one-eighth Irish," he answered.

As my eyebrows furrowed, I listened to him explain that his grandfather—a fiery, redheaded, full-blooded Irishman—had married a calm and sensible German woman. His father did the same.

One-eighth Irish? Picturing my body divided into eight parts, that just about covered my right knee, calf, ankle, and foot. The truth about my paltry Irish fraction left me disheartened. How could I ever call myself Irish again? My Dad, a man of few words and great intuition, supplied an answer.

"All you need is a drop," he said.

At the time, those words provided little comfort. Today, they make sense.

I believe my Irish comes out every day when I'm writing or sharing stories, flashing my green eyes, and smiling at strangers. My late dad's spirit is right beside me, along with all the other Ryans in our family tree who toiled, laughed, and loved before me.

To honor my dad and our Irish heritage, I passed on the family name to my son. John Ryan Martin is one-sixteenth Irish. But it doesn't matter...

All you need is a drop.

Chere Are No Strangers

by Brendan P. Myers

hen I was in college, I spent one summer exploring the west coast of Ireland with some friends. Unable to get on the same flight home as my friends, I spent the next few days traveling around on my own. That's how I found myself at a pub in Tralee.

There were no empty seats at the bar, so I sat at a table occupied by a young couple and a teenage boy. The boy quickly introduced himself and his sister before proudly introducing his "future brother-in-law." The couple looked relieved the boy had found himself a new distraction. They sent a nod my way before returning to gaze into each other's eyes.

The boy just kept talking. His name was Tim, and for the next few hours he told me about his favorite books, his teachers, and the posters of Irish heroes that adorned the walls of his bedroom. He talked excitedly about his sister's upcoming wedding in which he was to be best man.

I mostly smiled and nodded and tried to keep up. Yet for some reason, I found the kid oddly familiar. Maybe he just reminded me of myself at his age. Or maybe it was simply, as my own mother said so often about me, he had the map of Ireland on his face.

As it neared eleven thirty, he asked me a question. "Do you have family roots in Ireland?"

"Yes, I do," I answered. I smiled to recall my recent visit to the town my family had come from. While there, I stopped inside the church, where generations before me had been baptized and married, and visited the graves of long-lost relatives. I was the first in three generations of my family to return to Ireland.

"Wher're they from?" he asked.

"Castle Island," I answered.

His eyes went wide.

"Castle Island! That's where I'm from. What's the family name?" he asked.

"Coffey," I answered. His eyes went wider still.

"That's my name!" he said, "Timmy. Timmy Coffey!"

After saying our goodbyes, I remembered my strange sense of familiarity with the kid, the almost spooky feeling we had met before. And as I walked back to my hotel, I recalled this quote often attributed to William Butler Yeats: "There are no strangers here, only friends you haven't yet met." And sometimes, I thought, family.

It is often when we are not searching
that we find the most valuable treasures.

Food, Music, and Friends from the Old Country

by Rosemary Dolan Lesh

y parents were Irish immigrants, and while we didn't have a lot of money, we did have wonderful holidays with great food, drink, and a house full of company. I especially remember St. Patrick's Day when friends and relatives would come on buses from all parts of Chicago to our South Side home.

Two o'clock was the typical arrival time for company, so Mom would tell me to keep a look out the window starting about one thirty for any early birds. I would crane my neck against the window, peering way down the street, and then upon seeing some familiar faces, I would holler at the top of my lungs, "Here come the Kilcoynes!" Then, "Here comes Uncle Mike!" and "Here are the Cassidys!" This would go on and on until we soon had a houseful of guests laughing, drinking, and speaking with their various brogues from all over Ireland.

Eventually, Mom would call us all over to the table for one of her wonderful home-cooked meals with so many dishes they filled the whole table. Her yeast rolls were what really drove everyone wild—light as a feather and still warm from the oven, the butter would run down our chins. My three older brothers could eat dozens of them themselves, and Mom would always have to warn them to leave some for the guests.

After dinner we would take to our beds for a "wee nap" only to get up a few hours later for Mom's even more famous strawberry shortcake with real whipped cream, lemon meringue pie, and a pot of tea.

In the evening, the company would sit in the living room for more chatting, and soon, for everyone's enjoyment, my brother Francie would be summoned to sing some of the great old Irish songs, such as "I'll Take You Home Again, Kathleen" and "The Stone Outside Dan Murphy's Door."

Then, one by one and couple by couple, our guests would put on their coats and say goodbye, with the promise that we would all convene again next year, "God willing."

Now, many years later, it's nice to think back on those days of youth and innocence when my parents and their friends from the "old country" filled our home with warmth, love, and much laughter, renewing friendships in their new, adopted country. These wonderful days attested to the old Irish adage...

Let your house be too small
to hold all of your friends.

Some Things Never Change

by Herb Shallcross

t's a good thing my mom is always right, because she sure is stubborn. Whether it is advice for life or the only way to prepare her favorite Irish dish, she always makes her opinions strikingly clear.

When I was twelve, I asked my mom why we always ate potatoes. Irish tradition, she told me. She explained that potatoes are one of the few crops that flourished in Ireland's climate. She said that many people in Ireland relied on potatoes for sustenance, so much so that potato famines led to widespread starvation.

Strangely, she was finicky when it came to potatoes. She refused to eat skins on mashed potatoes. This seemed to be at odds with the history she had just recounted to me.

"Then why do you always make your mashed potatoes without the skins?" I asked. "Isn't that where most of the nutrients are?"

She stopped, stumped. She seemed to have a revelation: she was giving us the appearance of cultural traditions, but not the sustenance. But who could blame her? She had not really experienced the culture herself. My mother had not been to Ireland except when she toured Europe in her twenties.

So perhaps it was potato skins that prompted my mom to take her second journey to Ireland at the age of fifty-five. She and my father experienced her homeland and brought back true stories of how people lived there.

I have never seen my mom smile wider than when she returned. She was exactly the vibrant, wide-eyed young woman I had imagined when she told me about her first trip to Ireland. She talked and talked as we all sat down to enjoy a big meal of steak and potatoes she had cooked.

Mom may have been inspired by her trip, but she was not changed: the mashed potatoes came out a creamy, pure-white mound, skinless as usual. I no longer try to convince her to change.

If you wish to change the mind
of a stubborn Irish person, good luck.
You might as well be
whistling jigs to a milestone!

A Traditional Irish Dish: Champ

by Katherine Nolan

hamp is simplicity itself to make and is the greatest comfort food imaginable—except maybe for its close relative, Colcannon. This is food for a cold winter's day, a dish to nurse a cold or to mend a broken heart—whatever ails you will not seem so bad when you tuck into a great bowlful of champ... It's so simple it barely counts as a recipe!

> 2 pounds potatoes, or about 4-6 large potatoes ("Old" potatoes or Russet potatoes are best; waxy potatoes won't do.)
> ½ cup milk
> 1 stick butter, divided into two parts
> 5-6 scallions, chopped
> Salt and pepper
> Fresh parsley

Yes, I know it is a lot of butter, but you really cannot skimp with champ!

Peel and boil the potatoes until they are quite soft. When the potatoes are done, drain and return the saucepan, with the drained potatoes in, to a low burner, leaving the lid off so that any excess moisture can evaporate. When they are perfectly dry, add the milk to the saucepan along with half the butter and the chopped scallions. Allow the milk to warm but not boil—it is about right when the butter has fully melted into it and it starts to steam.

With a potato masher or a fork, mash the potatoes thoroughly into the butter/milk mixture. Do not pass through a ricer or, worse, beat in a mixer as it will make the potatoes gluey and disgusting. Mix the scallions thoroughly into the mashed potatoes. Season to taste with salt and pepper.

Before serving, sprinkle with fresh chopped parsley. Most importantly, make a well in the center of the potato in each serving and put a good pat of butter in it to melt. Eat by dipping forkfuls of potato into the melting well of butter. The world will seem a better place.

Laughter is brightest where food is best.
— Irish proverb

A Trip to Tuosist

by David Yeadon

"I wouldn't be parking there if I w' you," said the white-haired lady at the post office door. She reminded me of my Irish grandmother—tightly bunned hair, frowny, strict expression hiding a reluctant smile, and a determined manner that forbade contradiction or even the slightest hint of a question.

But I did have a question. After our dramatic nail-biting drive over the switchback challenge of the Healy Pass, I'd parked across the road from her tiny post office/grocery store at Tuosist, which despite its nebulous size, is the key parish of the County Kerry section of the Beara, stretching twenty-three miles from Kenmare to Ardgroom. I'd parked on a grass verge off the winding narrow back road and well away from the frantic antics of Cork drivers. Not that there were any around here. We hadn't seen a car for miles.

"You don't think it's okay here?"

"That's what I jus' said," she replied sternly.

"Well—we're just coming into your store for a minute. I'm sure it'll be fine."

"Is that so, y'think?" was all she replied before she vanished inside.

We followed her, bought a couple of oranges and some oversugary Brit candies... We explained to the lady (still unsmiling) that we were looking for Tuosist parish hall. We'd heard from Jim O'Sullivan that there was some kind of annual festival of local folklore and other regional peculiarities going on over there.

"Well now, y'jus passed it. It's barely fifty yards away," she said, regarding us skeptically as hapless tourists. "There it is." She came to the door and pointed from the corner of the post office down a lane to a small school building with a substantial whitewashed depiction of the Crucifixion towering twelve feet over the road. "Don't know how you could have missed that."

"Looks like we're not going to miss this, though," gasped Anne as round the corner from our parked car came a herd of thirty or so cattle swaying, lumbering, and mooing through the mud and constantly trying to break free from the ankle-nipping dogs controlling them. The post office lady was smiling now. Her face creased and wrinkled with mirth and a defiant look of "Now didn't I tell y'so?"

From the cows' point of view, our car was obviously an obstacle to be enjoyed—a way to escape the dogs. So they rubbed and scrunched against it, tried to hide behind it, or ran circles around it, all the while churning up ribbons of mud and murky grime from the soggy grass verge and relieving themselves copiously along their erratic ways. When they'd finally been corralled and moved on down the lane it was rather difficult to distinguish our previously bright and shiny silver rented Opal from all the mire and muck surrounding it.

We had to laugh. "Well—I guess your advice was good," I said as we tried to remove the goo from the door handles. At this point, God bless her, the post office lady finally let her warm Irish heart show through her stern carapace. "No—wait a minute now. Let me get you a bucket and a cloth. You'll never get all that stuff off with your fingers—the idea of it!"

So giggling, she brought the water and cloths for us to wash it back to something recognizable as a car.

A light heart lives long.
— Irish proverb

"Rush Hour"

by Gina Wynne

 t is rush hour in Connemara. Our four wheels creep to a stop on the Irish blacktop that's been curling us through the foggy countryside all morning. We crank down the windows and crane our necks out to get a better look at the roadblock. Sheep. It looks like a bundle of sweaters waddling across the road, and it seems as if they are casually discussing their pastures on the way to get a cup of coffee. Fifteen maybe twenty of them slowly clog into the greener grass on the other side, and we wait for the stragglers to catch up before putting the car in gear. The shaggy commuters head off into the mist, leaving us to wonder where their work takes them. Whatever it is, it will be there when they get there. Eventually.

Take the world nice and easy,
and the world will take you the same.

— Irish saying

In an Irish State of Mind

by Beth Wallach

 like to think of Ireland as a state of mind—
something longed for when not there and a
place that soothes the modern-day soul when
you walk its streets, hear its music, drink
its spirits, and come up against its unrelenting wind.
It's in the ruddiness of the men's faces walking down
O'Connell Street during rush hour. It's in the worn
fingers of the fiddle player and in the tattered shoes of
the toe-tapping accordionist. It's in its perseverance in
the face of a blood-soaked history and eventual partition.
And it's in the immortal words of its storytellers.

It's in the endless miles of stone walls as you traverse
the country from end to end. It's in its impossible road
signs that point you in one direction yet lead you in
another. It's in its castles from Bunratty to Blarney and
on its roadways from Connemara to Kerry. It's in a
jaunting car ride through misty skies in the Gap of
Dunloe and getting lost in a book curled up by a fire at an
inn in Westport... and everywhere it's in the color green.

May your mind be filled with pleasant thoughts...
and may those thoughts be of the Emerald Isle.

The Weather in West Clare

by Thomas Lynch

"Grand day thank God," is what the Moveen crowd says whenever they wake to anything within the range of tolerable miseries.

"Not as bad as the night of the Debbie," is what they'll say when slates fly off the house, or the power goes down, or the rain makes a puddle out of everything. It was August 1969 when Hurricane Debbie rose up out of the Caribbean and made its way across the North Atlantic to sweep hay barns and knock some ancient walls in West Clare.

"Grand day thank God," is what they mostly say, grateful to be up and out in it. Or "soft day," or "it's very broken." One rarely hears the out-and-out complaint that the weather in West Clare is severely damaged compared to, say, Cuba or Connecticut or Melbourne or East Clare, where trees can stand and gardens thrive and people can go about their business.

More menacing than the forty days of rain in every month of every season, and the gale-force winds that pound the place, are those odd stretches, known to go weeks on end, of unseasonably kindly weather—the sweet breath of the Antilles in the air, so gentle on the skin that the skin rejoices, the light so magic that the eye can hardly bear such beauty, the heart aching with thanksgiving for the day that's in it.

I've seen it hit in March or April or November and once near the feast of St. Serenus, in late February. The day-trippers come in their cars to Kilkee. The seafront lodges fill with weekenders. The merchants open for unexpected trade. The pubs grant themselves a dispensation. Everyone thinks of it as a bonus.

For the first few days there is the usual greeting, punctuated with authentic glee. "Grand day thank God, entirely!" But after several days in the one week of such relief, the locals take a different view, knowing as sure as heaven there's hell to pay and that too much good requires much more bad to balance it.

"Grand day," they say with the wary look of the long-suffering, waiting out old peril and new doom, "Grand day, indeed, the Lord've mercy on us all."

There are no unmixed blessings in life.
— Irish proverb

Romancing a Stone
by A. G. McEvoy

ave you ever wanted to dangle upside down eighty feet in the air to kiss a rock? If you want to kiss the Blarney Stone, that is exactly what you get to do.

The Blarney Stone sits atop Blarney Castle located near the city of Cork in Southern Ireland. Blarney Castle began as a hunting lodge in the 10th century. It was rebuilt in stone in 1210 only to be demolished and reconstructed by Dermot McCarthy in 1446.

There are many legends surrounding the history of the Blarney Stone itself. One old tale states that one of Dermot's ancestors, Cormac McCarthy, King of Munster, saved an old woman from drowning. The woman was actually a witch. As a reward, she told him of a secret stone in the castle. Anyone who kissed the stone would be given "the gift of eloquence" or as the locals say, "the gift of the gab."

Getting to the top of the castle where the stone is located, however, is not free of some hardship. The castle is mostly in ruins. The spiral staircase is narrow and steep, providing only one way up and down. It was built this way to ensure the safety of its residents because, should an invasion occur, only one invader at a time could come up the staircase.

Once you get to the top of the eighty-foot castle where the stone is located, you do not get to just stand there and pucker up. Oh no! Now you must lie on your back and reach out to grab two iron railings attached to the parapet, which is a lower wall on the outside of the main wall. While you grip the railings you lower yourself down about two feet and lay your best kiss on the Blarney Stone, which is also on the parapet. Although there is a small grate below you and someone there to hold on to you, anyone with a fear of heights may want to abandon this adventure altogether.

But if heights do not bother you, you will enjoy not only receiving the "gift of the gab" but the breathtaking countryside you can see from atop the castle. Blarney Castle is situated in over a thousand acres of magnificent woodland, making it the ideal place to take walks and enjoy the fresh air.

Over 200,000 people visit the castle each year. As it is a very popular tourist spot, it is a good idea to go either early or late in the day to avoid the many tour buses.

So if you wish to become an eloquent speaker, you can practice your diction... or you can take a trip to Blarney Castle and try kissing an ancient stone that may make your dream come true!

Those with adventurous hearts
may find life a little more magical.

Little Women's Christmas

by Sheila Flitton

"*ollaig na mBan*" or "Little Women's Christmas" is an old custom that's still celebrated by women all over Ireland. It goes back to the days when large families were the norm. Men never lifted a finger in the house to help and were never expected to. If a man washed the dishes, he would be called an "auld woman" by other men. No full-blooded Irishman was prepared to risk that!

But each year, after the Christmas holiday, tired women finally got a break—for one day, at least. On January 6 (the same day as the Epiphany), men would take over the housework, offering women a chance to relax with each other.

Never one to break with tradition, I returned to my hometown of Cork this year (from Dublin) to join my sisters and women friends to celebrate. As we sat overlooking the River Lee from Cork's Metropole Hotel dining room, I thought, "We keep the tradition alive, but not in the same way our mothers did."

During my childhood, I remember excited, shawled women hurrying to the local public house. On Little Women's Christmas, they would inhabit this man's domain without shame. Sitting in "the snug," a small private room inside the front door, they would pool the few shillings they'd saved for the day. Then they would drink stout and dine on thick corned beef sandwiches provided by the publican. For the rest of the year, the only time respectable women would meet for a glass of stout would be during shopping hours, and then only because it was "good for iron in the blood."

After an initial chat about the worries and cares of the old year, a pact would be made to leave them outside the door (something that was easier to do before the advent of cell phones). They'd be as free as the birds in the sky for the day—and well on into the evening. Late at night, with shawls dropped over their shoulders, words slurred and voices hoarse, they would always sing. In my memory, I still hear them bellowing the unofficial Cork City anthem, "The Banks of My Own Lovely Lee":

> Where they sported and played
> 'neath the green leafy shade
> on the banks of my own lovely Lee.

Some say this tradition is dying, but I was surprised to see how many women of all ages upheld it this year. Like my own sisters and friends, most women no longer gather in the snug of a public house. Wine and lunch have replaced the bottle of stout and corned beef sandwiches. And of course, today's new man, no stranger to the kitchen, is home trying his hand at cooking and spending quality time with the children (or so he says). We can't stop progress, but it's a pleasure to see Little Women's Christmas survive.

Some traditions are worth keeping alive.

The Rocks of Creg Bherige

by Anne Kelly

We played here as small children
Exploring the crevices and tunnels
Finding mysterious hiding places
Dark enough but not too frightening.

Always on the edge of adventure
Crawling into the foxes' dens
Peering out through rabbit's eyes
Covering ourselves in grey granite.

Sometimes we achieved a breakthrough
Climbing up a twisted chimney
Squeezing through the rocks
Bursting out into bright sunshine.

Often we stayed quite still inside
The rock castle acting as a shield.
We listened to our mother's voices
Mingling with the music of the sea.

Days and weeks saving turf on the bog
Relieved by the magic of Creg Bherige,
Crawling out on to the heather
Catching the scent of bog flowers.

The rocks yielded inner hiding places
Where we could be our different selves
Giving us shade in the sunshine
And shelter in the driving rain.

We tumbled out on to the soft green circle
Laughing and playing aloud
The secret magic of the rock structure
And the soft green circle still call me back.

Childhood Memories in
White Park Bay

by Sheelagh McKay

s a child, I lived in a place called Port
Braddon at White Park Bay. Ours was the
first house as you came down the hairpin
bends. "Carrick Inan" was its name, and it
must be close to four hundred years old now. Our home
was always filled with laughter, animals (our own as
well as strays), and music.

In spring, the farmer McCurdy's cows from up
the road used to love our big front lawn. They let
themselves in through the gate, leaving great soggy
hoofprints over my dad's pride and joy and eating my
mom's just-sprouting flowers. They took no notice
of our untrained sheepdog Queenie's increasingly
outraged efforts to herd them up the road!

In summer, the doors would be flung wide and my
Aunt Ivy's piano playing could be heard clear across
the bay to Ballintoy. We'd spend the long summer and
autumn days outside in the garden or on White Park
Bay. I clearly remember picking blackberries... and
coming home black-stained, tired, scratched, and happy
to find sterilized jam jars glistening and waiting for
jam making.

In winter, we would snuggle happily under Carrick
Inan's protective roof and watch the snow lay thick
white blankets over everything. The icicles hanging

from the cliffs above the hairpin bends were taller than my dad. Relatives, neighbors, and friends would arrive unannounced to join us for a "wee sherry" or a glass of old Bushmills. Out would come the accordion, and with Ivy's piano playing, the songs and laughter would have me dancing and singing along with the adults. I was always so sad to have to go to bed and leave them to it.

My childhood was filled with fairies and long golden evenings, playing around the lupines, splashing in the back garden burn, going out in the boat with my uncle, Bertie McKay, and catching great boatfuls of silvery, splashing salmon that left me covered in shiny scales.

Sadly, my Port Braddon days became memories when, at the age of seven, I left to live in Zimbabwe. Carrick Inan is mine in possession no more, but in my heart it will always belong to me. Now, ten years of living in South Africa is coming to an end, and I prepare myself to return to the place where I have always belonged and been free... Ireland.

It is true: once the spirit of Ireland is in your blood, it will always call you home.

Things Remembered

by Annabel Davis-Goff

have chosen to live my adult life away from my own country. Despite nostalgia and even occasional homesickness, it is not a choice I regret. But there is a deep feeling of peace which starts when the airplane gets close enough to the land for me to see not only the essential damp greenness of Ireland but that the trees grow lopsided, their irregular shapes formed by the prevailing wind. Recognition and memory. Going home. It would be sentimental and untrue to say that I have more in common with my average countryman than I have with my friends in New York. Not more or even as much, but something. Something small and important. Memory and knowledge. Knowing what an Irish country summer evening sounds and looks and smells like. A memory of a December morning with a light frost—frozen mud white-crested underfoot and pale sunshine. New-mown hay or apples slightly overripe after their winter in the slatted wooden storage racks. Some of this occurs in the exact form I remember only in Ireland. Most of it, of course, can happen anywhere. But the smell of tomatoes every year in our garden in Connecticut reminds me, not of the previous summer, but of my father in the greenhouse nipping off the small, pungent, green shoots between a stained thumbnail and forefinger. There is a feeling of relief which, I suppose, comes from knowing that I am

among people who make the same associations with
the sea, a gentle rain, and the sounds of corncrakes
and crows.

Sea pinks and Christmas roses. The Angelus. Cowslips
and salmon ladders. Crumbling Georgian houses and
solid ancient ruins. Overgrown canals and miles of empty
wide golden beaches. Fuchsia growing wild in the hedges
of West Cork—a deeper, richer red than any fancy New
York florist can ever offer. The other side of the same
dusty August road a hedge of honeysuckle and wild roses.
A gap—through a crooked handmade gate—shows a pond
covered with water lilies. Giant oak trees, soft green
beeches with nuts below on the moss, horse chestnuts
with shiny conkers, mountain ash but also the treeless
solid green and rock headlands out into the Atlantic with
the occasional ruin breaking the flat line. Wild orchids.
Fairy rings and hedgehogs. Turf fires. Sweaters made of
unwashed wool—waterproof, slightly greasy and smelling
a little of sheep until washed. Irish coins, each with a
harp on one side and an animal on the reverse—a hen on
the vast copper penny—a pig, a hare, a greyhound, a bull,
a horse and a salmon on the silver.

Our memories of home stay with us no matter how
far we may wander.

Coming Home
by Donna Duly Volkenannt

t Fourth of July family picnics, as fireworks out-sparkled stars in the nighttime sky, I heard about how my great-grandfather and his family fled Ireland during the "Potato Famine." While I munched watermelon and drank grape soda, Dad told stories about Michael Duly's journey across the Atlantic on a "coffin ship."

Dad told me, "When he arrived in America, Michael's brogue was so thick they couldn't understand him. That's why our name is spelled D-u-l-y and not D-o-o-l-e-y."

Uncle Mike, Dad's oldest brother and my great-grandfather's namesake, shared a different tale. "Truth be told, Michael's father changed the spelling because he got into a 'spot of trouble' with the English and didn't want to be found."

Other relatives told their own versions of Michael's story. Yet, one fact they all agree on was my great-grandfather's wish to return to the land of his birth. Sadly, Michael died before he could make the trip.

When I asked Uncle Mike to tell me more about my Irish roots, he told me, "Michael lived in New York before he got a job with the railroad and headed west. After he got to Missouri, he became a farmer and married Susan O'Donnell." Uncle Mike also gave me directions to the church graveyard where Michael and Susan are buried.

One summer afternoon, my husband, Walt, and I drove to the small country church in rural Missouri. The sun bore down and bees droned around the wrought iron fence that circled the well-kept grounds. The smell of honeysuckle and wild roses filled the air as I spotted a large Celtic cross in the old section of the graveyard. An inscription on the Duly stone detailed Michael's birth. He was born on St. Patrick's Day in King's County, Ireland—facts I never knew. Before leaving, I took photos to capture the moment and record a piece of family history.

A few years later my sisters and I decided to visit Ireland. In preparation for our trip, I researched King's County and discovered it was renamed Offaly County. Before our departure, I returned to the Duly gravesite, where I scooped up soil to carry on my pilgrimage to Ireland.

At Clonmacnoise Monastery in Offaly County, chills danced across my shoulders as I stood on a hillside overlooking the River Shannon. While reciting a prayer, I scattered soil from Michael's gravesite onto the ground in the county where his life began.

Back on the bus, a peaceful presence settled over me. I realized how blessed I am to have ancestors who braved starvation and death to begin life anew in a foreign land. I smiled and remembered how my father's family cherished its roots and delighted in telling stories—regardless of the facts.

After returning to Missouri, my heart filled with joy when I sprinkled earth from Ireland at the foot of the Duly family cross. Although Michael never fulfilled his dream of returning to the Emerald Isle, three generations later a small portion of Eire came home to rest near him.

Through the grace of God, our roots
will guide us home.

Inheriting Irish Values

by Diane Loftus

y lovely grandparents were from the untamed west coast of Ireland from the County of Mayo. As my father described it to me, it was the land of enchantment, fairies, leprechauns, and many dreams. My dad taught me the *craic*, a bit of the blarney, and the love of the Irish and what it meant to him. As a lass, I grew up loving Ireland, the Irish people, and the wonderful Irish tunes. My father told me long ago that the tunes were the Irish way of telling their life history.

My dad's father paid his passage to the USA by singing, dancing, and playing his squeeze box on his journey across the wild, roaring ocean. My father passed on to me what was taught to him by two emigrant parents and their love for their country and their countrymen. As my father would say, "Ireland 'tis a wee bit of heaven."

I am from a family of ten children, and my father worked hard for all of us and stood beside us through thick and thin. He loved us more than life itself and would fight for us more than heavyweight boxer Jack Dempsey. My father was at every school, sports, and church event there was. When I grew up, we didn't have much, yet we grew up thinking we were no better or no less than others were.

I thank my dad for teaching us his values and the values of his parents. He had a heart of gold that the leprechauns would have envied, and his family was more precious to him than a pot of gold. Part of my dad lives on in me and in my children... and someday in my grandchildren.

My father taught me to be a strong, proud Irishwoman, and I live by his words of wisdom daily. There is not one day that goes by that I don't think about the man and sometimes smile to myself about things he said or did. One of the wonderful things I remember him telling me is this...

Know that if you can make it
through one more day
and live it to the fullest
and be the best you can be,
you will always be strong,
happy, and healthy.

Leaving Beara for the First Time

by David Yeadon

e really don't want to leave. Particularly on a day like this. After almost a week of miserable gray glop, our last morning of the spring season on Beara, and the dawn is crisp-clear. Within an hour, the sky is pigeon-egg blue dappled with tiny white curlicues of cloud. The Skelligs are there too, no longer playing hide-and-seek in the sea hazes, but bold and proud as galleons—seemingly close enough to us to stroke their razored, almost reptilian ridges.

The tall grasses along the stream are swaying in the faintest of breezes, the buttercups beaming with a gilded sheen, and the daisies virginal white and nodding like a happy host of behatted schoolgirls. (Forgive the overindulgent imagery, but I was feeling rather Wordsworthian that morning.) Behind us are the rugged remnants of the tin mines, the chimneys and stone-walled engine houses, broken and black against the brittle summits and strangely eroded flanks of the hills.

Over a fold in the half-moor of abandoned fields with their collapsing walls peeps the gaudy strip of houses, pubs, and shops of Allihies. The carnival cacophony of colors seems almost too blushingly self-conscious, especially as across the rest of the sweeping landscape bound by high ridges, most of the cottages and farms are demurely white or, at their most flamboyant, a delicate shade of lemony cream. This is a color echoed in the broad sweep of our sand beach, that unexpected bonus of copper ore tailings once washed down to the sea from the mines up on the hill. And then—of course—come the greens of the fields and pastures and inbye plots in a patch-work quilt of fervent late spring fertility. You could spend a year painting these and still not exhaust the patterned permutations of green in every imaginable tone and hue.

And as the sun begins its daily arc, the land seems to change shape constantly. The slowly moving shadows expose a welter of bumps and lumps that could be—and in most instances actually are—anything from ancient neolithic ring forts or stone circles to more recent ruins of the old "famine-era" houses, tumbled in tirades of wrath by avaricious eviction-lusting landlords or merely long collapsed through structural fatigue and the ever-increasing weight of sodden, mold-ridden thatch.

One thing is obvious from all these shadowy presences—this has been an active, well-used land, far more populous than today. And when the mists float across these bumps and lumps here and when the twilight blurs edges and diffuses things, you can often sense the soft sussurus, the eerie echoes of layered existences.

And we shall miss them—all of them. And we shall miss even the gray glop days when those proud Skelligs vanish and the unshorn sheep look like bags of rags scattered among the gorse and marsh grass. We shall miss our Beara. Very much.

It is hard to say goodbye to something of such beauty.

Making Ireland
Your Home

by Steenie Harvey

A new life in Ireland. Sounds like a wonderful idea, but is it really possible? Well, I'd just like to tell you that dreams can come true. I should know, mine did.

I haven't always been a writer... And Ireland is my adopted home, rather than my place of birth. Back in the late 1980s, my life was in a rut. I lived in a dreary industrial English town and had an equally dreary job as an office clerk in a printing factory.

Although family life was great—wonderful husband, wonderful daughter—I felt crushed by the sheer grind of my day-to-day existence. I got up, went to work, caught a bus home, cooked dinner, and watched television. Day after day after day. But what's wrong with that? After all, thousands of people were in the same boat as me.

Then a bombshell dropped—my husband, Michael, lost his job. Maybe it was the shock of discovering our income had been cut in half, but we had this crazy idea. Why not move away, try a completely different lifestyle?

We knew Ireland, having spent several vacations there—and Michael has Irish blood passed down from his grandfathers. We had always enjoyed fantastic holidays in Ireland, and it seemed such a gentle place, so why not give it a try? I had always yearned to live in the countryside, and Ireland certainly had plenty of that...

It's hard to believe now, but we went to Ireland with the idea of buying a home for less than $15,000. It took some months of searching, but we did eventually hit gold. We found a cozy cottage overlooking Lough Key in County Roscommon. This was just how I'd pictured country living: a huge garden where we could grow all our own vegetables, room enough to have a dog and three cats, a shop, and a couple of excellent pubs—all within a mile's walk. Plus we were surrounded by lovely neighbors—and, by the way, I can assure you that all those things you may have heard about Irish warmth and hospitality are true...

Seventeen years on, we're still living in the same little cottage. Our daughter has married an Irishman, and we've acquired a bunch of grandkids—six in total. ("What are you trying to do?" I ask her. "Repopulate the west of Ireland all by yourself?") And my writing career has soared... Not only have I had books published, I also spend a fair bit of time traveling around Europe on behalf of an American magazine, writing about real estate. Would this have happened if I hadn't moved to Ireland? Don't think so. Chances are I'd still be on the other end of a telephone, explaining to irate customers why their printing orders weren't ready.

But here's the thing: I've never been tempted to move on again. Flying back from Portugal a week ago, the same tremendous thrill swept through me that I felt the first time I ever visited Ireland. My heart always lifts as the plane swoops over Dublin Bay, and once again I see my adopted homeland emerging from the mist.

I think what I'm trying to say is this: I love this country, and I can't imagine any reason why I'd want to say goodbye... I very much hope that you too will come and experience the magic. It may be just for a visit, but then again...

Ireland and its enchantments
may keep you here forever.

I Am of Achill

by Anne Kelly

I am of Achill
The sea and mountains,
Rivers, lakes, fields,
Flowers, fences,
Rocks, pebbles, stones,
Cliffs, wells, springs,
Heather, fuchsia, gorse
Rough terrain and smooth
All are part of me.

I am of Achill
Achill people formed me
My father bent his back in England
My mother picked potatoes in Scotland
Relatives of mine broke stones
In quarries as far away
As America and South Africa.
All Achill people
Achill to the bone.

You are of Achill
Your people lie in Kildownet
Or further west in Sliabh Mor
Your sons and daughters travel
To cities of distant shores
Achill paths were trodden
Long before Famine times
Fine musicians and singers
Voices still in the wind.

We are of Achill
Clouds, rainbows, rains,
Families exiled and scattered
People on ships and planes.
People with cherished memories
Who never feel far away
From the tones and textures of Achill
From the tang of Atlantic spray.

I am of Achill
Memories in ancient ruins
Houses and lands deserted
Villages speaking in stones.
Blending of winds and waters
Soft mists and cold brown clay.
We are the people of Achill
Whether we go or stay.

The Real Ireland

by Dan Barry

n August night in the sea-scented village of Kinvara finds us at Connolly's, a pub so permanent that if some codger were to tell you it was here before Galway Bay, lapping now just outside the door, you'd nod and buy him a pint. My wife and I are hunched at a small table with friends when a smiling woman in a peasant skirt sits beside us, carrying a perfectly appropriate accessory in this corner of Ireland—a button accordion.

She is Mary Staunton, a musician known throughout the Irish west. When the inevitable call goes out, she obliges, her fingers skipping across the buttons like children playing frantic but sure-footed hopscotch. Then a white-haired man mentions an old song from his childhood. Does she know it? Why yes, she does, and when her fingers finish their dance, leaving the man smiling, there suddenly rises from across the room the hesitant but clear voice of a young woman who has summoned the nerve to sing. ("And I said let grief be a fallen leaf/At the dawning of the day.") As she sings, all talking stops: an entire pub, transported. And I think to myself, now this would never happen where I'm from…

Over the years, I have spent a lot of time in the western counties of Galway and Clare, and if nothing else, this is what I have gleaned: Ireland can be that place you missed as you traveled around Ireland, looking for Ireland.

Yes, you can find a thatched cottage here and there, if you try. Yes, you may even encounter a white clot of sheep blocking your rented car's path, raising from musty memory some postcard caption about Irish Rush Hour. But to wander about, looking to bag with a digital camera some approximation of a time-faded Irish postcard, is to miss the complexities of a country that is thoroughly enjoying its wealth and adapting to its European Union membership while at the same time trying to preserve its dreamlike landscape and proud cultural heritage.

Though Kinvara is perfectly situated for day trips to other points of the Irish west, I often struggle with whether to stay or to go, lulled as I am by the mundane daily rhythms of a village I have come to know in all seasons.

In the mornings, I watch the same white-bearded fisherman—said to be Kinvara's last—park his old black bicycle by the pier, row a skiff to his rusty-green vessel, and disappear into the bay. Sometime later I see him rowing back to shore, where he mounts his bicycle and vanishes down a narrow lane, leaving me to wonder whether I had actually seen him or simply imagined him...

And in the evenings, I take walks with my wife and two young daughters along a worn path that meanders along the shoreline and through pastures where cows, horses, and donkeys approach, as if seeking the latest gossip from Connolly's... The sun drops, and somewhere voices are raised in song, seducing you to stay snug in Kinvara...

Another August night finds us with twenty others, talking and drinking under an awning outside the Pier Head, a bar and restaurant across the quay from Connolly's.

Those majestic boats called hookers rock gently in the bay. Dunguaire Castle, set aglow by floodlights, watches over Kinvara, as always. It is raining.

Then a man I know starts singing, as is his habit at moments like these. With eyes closed, he sings an old song written by a Kinvara poet long gone, about the cuckoos calling from the woods within, and his love beside him and the tide full in. People fall quiet, many with heads bowed, creating a sense that in all of Ireland there are only these sounds: seawater lapping, rainwater tapping, and one man's song.

O, Ireland! O, Ireland!
We're never far apart,
For you and all your beauty
Fill my mind and touch my heart.
— Author unknown

ACKNOWLEDGMENTS

We gratefully acknowledge the permission granted by the following authors, publishers, and authors' representatives to reprint poems or excerpts from their publications.

The New York Times for "Hooked on a Single Place" by Christine S. Cozzens (*The New York Times*: May 18, 2003). Copyright © 2003 by *The New York Times*. All rights reserved.

Gotham Books, a division of Penguin Group (USA), Inc., for "A Round of Songs at a Pub in Rosscarbery" and "The Best Outlook on Life" from A COURSE CALLED IRELAND by Tom Coyne. Copyright © 2009 by Tom Coyne. All rights reserved.

New World Library, Novato, California, www.newworldlibrary.com, for "Paying Tribute to Irish Ancestors" from GLOBETROTTER DOGMA: 100 CANONS FOR ESCAPING THE RAT RACE AND EXPLORING THE WORLD by Bruce Northam. Copyright © 2007 by Bruce Northam. All rights reserved.

W. W. Norton & Company, Inc., for "In Yeats' Footsteps" and "The Weather in West Clare" from BOOKING PASSAGE by Thomas Lynch. Copyright © 2005 by Thomas Lynch. All rights reserved.

Katherine Nolan for "A Traditional Irish Dish: Champ" (Dochara.com: June 2008). Copyright © 2008 by Katherine Nolan. All rights reserved.

HarperCollins Publishers for "A Trip to Tuosist" and "Leaving Beara for the First Time" from AT THE EDGE OF IRELAND by David Yeadon. Copyright © 2009 by David Yeadon. All rights reserved.

Sheila Flitton for "Little Women's Christmas" (Ireland-Fun-Facts.com: February 2009). Copyright © 2009, 2010 by Sterling Scott Publishing. All rights reserved.

The Estate of Anne Kelly for "The Rocks of Creg Bherige" and "I Am of Achill" from Achill 24/7, www.achill247.com. Copyright © 2002 by Anne Kelly. All rights reserved.

Annabel Davis-Goff for "Things Remembered" from WALLED GARDENS. Copyright © 1989 by Annabel Davis-Goff. All rights reserved.

Avalon Travel Publishing, a division of Perseus Book Group, for "Making Ireland Your Home" from IRELAND: A TRAVELER'S TOOLS FOR LIVING LIKE A LOCAL by Steenie Harvey. Copyright © 2001 by Steenie Harvey. All rights reserved.

PARS International Corp. for "The Real Ireland" from "Does the Real Ireland Exist?" by Dan Barry (*The New York Times*: May 18, 2008). Copyright © 2008 by *The New York Times* used by permission and protected by the Copyright Laws of the United States. All rights reserved.

A careful effort has been made to trace the ownership of selections used in this anthology in order to obtain permission to reprint copyrighted material and give proper credit to the copyright owners. If any error or omission has occurred, it is completely inadvertent, and we would like to make corrections in future editions provided that written notification is made to the publisher:

BLUE MOUNTAIN ARTS, INC., P.O. Box 4549, Boulder, Colorado 80306.